DATE DUE

MAR 0 5 2002			
GAYLORD			PRINTED IN U.S.A.

United States Presidents

Abraham Lincoln

Anne Welsbacher

ABDO Publishing Company

visit us at
www.abdopub.com

Published by Abdo Publishing Company, 4940 Viking Drive, Edina, Minnesota 55435.
Copyright © 2001 by Abdo Consulting Group, Inc. International copyrights reserved in all
countries. No part of this book may be reproduced in any form without written permission
from the publisher.

Printed in the United States.

Photo Credits: Corbis

Contributing Editors: Bob Italia, Tamara L. Britton, Kate A. Furlong

Library of Congress Cataloging-in-Publication Data

Welsbacher, Anne, 1955-
    Abraham Lincoln / Anne Welsbacher.
      p. cm. -- (United States presidents)
    Includes index.
    Summary: A biography of the president who held the country together during the bloodiest
war ever fought in the United States.
    ISBN 1-56239-740-0
1. Lincoln, Abraham, 1809-1865--Juvenile literature. 2. Presidents--United States--Biography-
-Juvenile literature. [1. Lincoln, Abraham, 1809-1865. 2. Presidents.] I. Title. II. Series:
United States presidents (Edina, Minn.)
E457.905.W47   2001
973.7'092--dc21
[B]   97-51542
                                 CIP
                                 AC

Contents

Abraham Lincoln

Abraham Lincoln was the sixteenth president of the United States. He held the country together during the worst war ever fought in America.

Lincoln was honest and hard working. He was tall and thin, and liked to tell jokes, sometimes about himself! People called him Honest Abe.

Lincoln was the son of poor farmers. They lived in Indiana and Kentucky. Later, they moved to Illinois. Lincoln worked hard doing many chores. He did not attend much school, but he read every book he could find.

Lincoln had many jobs as a young man. He rode boats down the Mississippi River, worked in a store, and ran for public office. He lost the first time. But, he did not give up.

Later, Lincoln was elected a state legislator. He spoke out against slavery. He also worked as a lawyer and built a good practice. He was still poor, but he worked hard to repay his debts.

Lincoln married Mary Todd and had four sons. Two of his sons died while he was living.

Lincoln was elected a U.S. representative. He spoke out for freedom in many ways. His ideas made many people angry, but he fought for what he believed was right.

Abraham Lincoln was elected president of the United States. Eleven southern states decided to start their own country. They attacked the United States and began the Civil War.

Lincoln led the country through the hardest war in its history. His smart choices in battles helped the North defeat the South. He worked to preserve the country and gain freedom for slaves.

A few days after the Civil War ended, President Lincoln was shot and killed. Today, many people remember him as the greatest man in United States history.

An 1861 presidential portrait of Abraham Lincoln

Abraham Lincoln (1809-1865)
Sixteenth President

BORN:	February 12, 1809
PLACE OF BIRTH:	Hodgenville, Kentucky
ANCESTRY:	English
FATHER:	Thomas Lincoln (1778-1851)
MOTHER:	Nancy Hanks Lincoln (1784-1818)
STEPMOTHER:	Sarah Bush Johnston Lincoln (1788-1869)
WIFE:	Mary Todd (1818-1882)
CHILDREN:	Four boys
EDUCATION:	Local tutors; self-educated
RELIGION:	No formal affiliation
OCCUPATION:	Merchant, lawyer
MILITARY SERVICE:	Served in Illinois State Militia for 3 months during Black Hawk War (1832)
POLITICAL PARTY:	Republican

OFFICES HELD:	Member of Illinois Legislature; Member of U.S. House of Representatives
AGE AT INAUGURATION:	52
YEARS SERVED:	1861-1865, died in office
VICE PRESIDENT:	Hannibal Hamlin (1861-1865) and Andrew Johnson (1865)
DIED:	April 15, 1865, Washington, D.C., age 56
CAUSE OF DEATH:	Assassination

Birthplace of Abraham Lincoln

Early Years

*A*braham Lincoln was born in Hodgenville, Kentucky, on February 12, 1809. He was the second child of Thomas and Nancy Lincoln. He was named after his grandfather. Abraham's older sister Sarah was born in 1807. His younger brother Thomas was born in 1812, but lived only a few days.

In 1811, the Lincolns moved to Knob Creek. Abraham chopped wood, planted crops, and carried water. When he wasn't working, he liked to explore the woods, climb the cliffs, and sit looking at the trees around him.

When Abraham was six, he and his sister went to school for a while. He learned to read, write, and do math. In 1816, his family moved to Indiana.

On October 5, 1818, Abraham's mother died. The next year, Abraham's father married a woman named Sarah Bush Johnston. She was called Sally. She had three children.

Sally soon noticed that Abraham liked to learn. She could tell he loved to read. Sometimes he walked miles to find a new book. At night, he sat close to the fire to read by its light. Sally helped Abraham continue his education. She gave him books and sent him to school when she could.

Abraham grew to be tall and strong. When he was caught up on chores at home, he worked on nearby farms to earn money. He always took a book with him.

Lincoln's birthplace in Kentucky

Honest Abe

*L*incoln soon got a job at Taylor's Mill. He **ferried** passengers across the Anderson River. When he was 19, Lincoln helped drive a boat down the Mississippi River to New Orleans. It was his first trip away from Indiana.

When he returned home, Lincoln helped his family move to Illinois. He and his father built a cabin and cleared fields. But, Lincoln had seen a different way of life in New Orleans. He wanted to set out on his own.

Lincoln ferries passengers across the Mississippi River.

10

In 1831, Lincoln helped drive another boat down the Mississippi River. The boat's owner, Denton Offutt, thought Lincoln did a good job. Offutt hired Lincoln to work in his store in New Salem, Illinois.

In 1832, Lincoln ran for the Illinois state **legislature**. He was a member of the **Whig** party. But, he stopped **campaigning** so he could join the Illinois state **militia**. He wanted to fight in the Black Hawk War. Lincoln was elected captain of his **company**. But, he was **discharged** without seeing combat. When he returned to New Salem, Lincoln lost the election for state legislator.

Lincoln decided to open a store with his friend William Berry. But the store soon went out of business. Then, Berry died. Lincoln was deeply in debt. So, he took a job as the town's postmaster. He also served as the town's **surveyor**. He made extra money doing odd jobs. He worked hard and paid all the money back. His honesty earned him the nickname Honest Abe.

A Young Lawyer

*I*n 1834, Lincoln again ran for the Illinois state **legislature**. This time he won. He was **re-elected** in 1836, 1838, and 1840. While in office, Lincoln worked to move Illinois's capital from Vandalia to Springfield. He also proposed the construction of railroads, highways, and canals to improve the state's transportation system. He favored creation of the United States Bank.

Lincoln studied law between legislative sessions. His friend John T. Stuart loaned him books and helped him study. He also walked to courthouses to listen to trials and watch lawyers and judges. Lincoln passed the bar exam, and received his law license on March 1, 1837. Then, he moved to Springfield.

Young Abraham Lincoln soon after becoming a lawyer

In 1839, Lincoln met Mary Todd. On November 4, 1842, they were married. They had four children. Robert was born in 1843, Edward in 1846, William in 1850, and Tad in 1853.

In 1844, the family moved into their own home. Lincoln and William H. Herndon started a law practice. They usually worked in Springfield. But twice a year, the court traveled to hear cases in **rural** counties.

Mary Todd Lincoln

Lincoln traveled Illinois's eighth **circuit** with the court. He became the regular lawyer for the Illinois Central Railroad. Lincoln was finally a successful businessman.

The Making of the
Sixteenth United States President

1809 → **1811** → **1816** → **1818** →

Born February 12 in Hodgenville, Kentucky

Moves to Knob Creek, Kentucky

Family moves to Indiana

Mother Nancy Hanks Lincoln dies

→ **1830** → **1831** → **1832** → **1834** →

Family moves to Illinois

Lincoln moves on his own to New Salem, Illinois

Runs for Illinois legislature and loses; joins militia

Elected to the Illinois legislature

→ **1846** → **1848** → **1850**

Elected to U.S. House of Representatives

Campaigns for Zachary Taylor

Four-year-old son Edward dies

1860

Elected president of the United States

Abraham Lincoln

"Four score and seven years ago our fathers brought forth on this continent, a new nation, conceived in liberty and dedicated to the proposition that all men are created equal."

1819
Father marries Sarah Johnston

➡ **1824**
Works as a hired farm hand

➡ **1828**
Drives cargo boat to New Orleans

Historic Events during Lincoln's Presidency

★ "In God We Trust" first appears on U.S. coins

★ Louis Pasteur invents pasteurization

★ The world's first subway opens in London, England

1837
Receives law license; moves to Springfield

➡ **1842**
Marries Mary Todd

➡ **1843**
The first of four sons is born

1861
The Civil War begins on April 12

1862
Son William dies

1863
Signs Emancipation Proclamation; gives Gettysburg Address

1864
Re-elected for second term

1865
Civil War ends; Lincoln is assassinated on April 15

PRESIDENTIAL YEARS

Freedom for All

*I*n 1846, Lincoln won a seat in the United States **House of Representatives**. He and his family moved into a boarding house in Washington, D.C.

During this time, people all over the country argued about whether or not slavery should be legal in the U.S. They also argued about whether new states should be free or have slavery.

While on a steamboat in 1831, Lincoln had seen slaves **shackled** together. This made him angry. So, Lincoln proposed a law to free the slaves in Washington, D.C. The government would pay slave owners for their release. But, Lincoln's law did not pass.

Lincoln fought for freedom in other ways, too. For example, he didn't think the U.S. should fight in the Mexican War. Lincoln believed the U.S. was unfairly taking land from Mexico.

Lincoln made speeches against the war. This angered many people. The U.S. won the war, and Mexico had to give up thousands of acres of land.

Lincoln also voted for a law called the Wilmot Proviso. It forbade slavery in the territory gained from Mexico. This law did not pass, either.

In 1848, Lincoln worked on Zachary Taylor's presidential **campaign**. Taylor won the election. Lincoln thought Taylor would make him **commissioner** of the land office in Illinois. But, Taylor gave the job to someone else. He offered Lincoln the job of governor of the Oregon Territory. But, Lincoln turned it down.

In 1849, Abraham Lincoln returned to his law practice in Springfield. In February 1850, his four-year-old son Edward died.

Zachary Taylor

A Bleeding Nation

*I*n 1854, Lincoln was **re-elected** to the Illinois state **legislature**. He gave up his seat so he could run for the Illinois **Senate**. But he was not chosen as a senator.

This same year, a law called the Kansas-Nebraska Act passed. It let the new states of Kansas and Nebraska decide whether to have slavery. It ended the Compromise of 1820, which had **banned** slavery in this area.

People in Kansas argued about whether to be slave or free. People who wanted slavery fought with those who didn't. Soon, people on each side were killing each other. During this time, the new state was called Bleeding Kansas.

Stephen A. Douglas

In 1856, Lincoln joined the new Republican party. This party was formed because of the Kansas-Nebraska Act. It was against slavery in the territories.

In 1858, Lincoln ran against Stephen A. Douglas for his seat in the U.S. Senate. Lincoln thought he could do a better job than Douglas. So, he asked Douglas to **debate** with him.

During the **debates**, Lincoln spoke against the Dred Scott decision. It supported slavery in the territories. Lincoln disagreed with this. He said, "A house divided against itself cannot stand." He thought the U.S. could not last being half slave and half free. Lincoln argued well against slavery, but he lost the election.

Republican party leaders had noticed Lincoln during the debates. They liked what he said. They nominated him for president in 1860. He ran against democratic **candidates** Douglas and John C. Breckinridge.

In November, Lincoln won the election. But the southern states did not like Lincoln's views on slavery. South Carolina **seceded** from the **Union**. To keep other states from seceding, **Congress** tried to pass the Crittenden Compromise. It said slavery would be legal in existing slave states. The territories would be divided between slave and free. The law did not pass. Six more states seceded. They formed the **Confederate States of America**.

In April, the Confederacy attacked Fort Sumter in South Carolina. With this attack, the Civil War began.

Fort Sumter after its surrender

President Lincoln

*L*incoln knew the Civil War would decide the future of the United States. He personally thought slavery was wrong and all people should be free. But, he felt the U.S. **Constitution** protected slavery in states where it already existed. His goal in the war was to preserve the Union.

In 1861, Lincoln blocked **ports** to Southern states. This made it hard for them to get supplies. He asked people to join the army. Soon, four more southern states **seceded** and joined the **Confederacy**.

In August 1861, Lincoln signed the first Confiscation Act. It allowed the **Union** army to take southern slaves that were involved in the war effort and use them for the military.

Lincoln also proposed that slaves in the **border states** be freed and their owners be paid $400 each for them. But, this did not become law. He also started the first income tax in American history.

Union States

Confederate States

Meanwhile, the war raged on. The **Confederacy** had a strong military with good leaders. It won many early battles. But the **Union** struggled to find an effective military leader. Winfield Scott, George B. McClellan, Ambrose Burnside, and Joseph Hooker all failed to lead the Union army successfully. So, Lincoln commanded the Union forces himself.

Ulysses S. Grant

Finally, General Ulysses S. Grant emerged as a strong leader. Despite setbacks at Bull Run and Shiloh, Grant became the leader of the Army of the West. But, Lincoln continued to direct all Union armies.

Lincoln believed the law protected slavery where it already existed. But, he did not want it to spread. So in June 1862, Lincoln signed a law that forbade slavery in unorganized territories. In July, he signed the second Confiscation Act. It freed all slaves in Confederate states whose owners had supported the war.

President Lincoln had spent much time thinking about the war and slavery. He knew that the slavery problem needed to be settled before the nation could have peace. But, he did not want to free all slaves right away. If he did, he feared the

Two escaped slaves

border states would **secede**. And, he was not sure where the freed slaves would live and work.

On September 22, 1862, Lincoln issued a **preliminary proclamation**. It said all slaves in the **Confederate** states would be freed in 100 days. Lincoln had added a new goal to the war. Besides saving the Union, he wanted to end slavery.

President Lincoln soon had new troubles. In December 1862, Sioux Native Americans who had been moved from their homelands in Minnesota attacked and killed white settlers. More than 300 Sioux were sentenced to die.

Lincoln did not think the Sioux got fair trials. He reviewed all the cases and decided that only 38 were guilty. His fairness saved many innocent lives.

Also in 1862, President Lincoln signed the Homestead Act. The act gave 160 acres (65 ha) of land to anyone who could farm the claim for five years. This allowed poor people in the east to own land in the west.

West Virginia seceded from Virginia and joined the **Union**. The Morrill Land-Grant College Act was passed. And, in February, Lincoln's son William died.

On January 1, 1863, President Lincoln signed the Emancipation Proclamation. It said all slaves in the **Confederate** states were free. He hoped that the **border states** would free their slaves, too. They did not. Still, slavery was ending.

Homesteaders heading west to stake their land claim under the Homestead Act

In 1863, the Union won the **Campaign** at Vicksburg and the Battle of Gettysburg. That November, President Lincoln gave a speech at the Gettysburg national cemetery.

The Gettysburg Address was short but strong. It said the "government of the people, by the people, for the people, shall not **perish** from the earth." The speech gave people hope that the states would stay together as one strong country.

In 1863, Lincoln signed laws that created a national banking system and military **conscription**. Thanksgiving became a national holiday. And, the **Union** began to take control of the war.

In 1864, **Union** General William T. Sherman captured Atlanta. The city was a major railroad center. It helped supply the **Confederate** army. After destroying Atlanta, Sherman began his march to Savannah.

President Lincoln won **re-election**. Included in his **platform** was the Thirteenth **Amendment** to the U.S. **Constitution**. This would outlaw slavery in the U.S. The amendment passed in **Congress**. It went to the states for **ratification**.

General William T. Sherman

Civil War
Battle Maps

Important Civil War sites in Virginia

In October, Nevada became a state. By December 22, Sherman had captured Savannah. Sherman's "March to the Sea" left a path of destruction all the way back to Atlanta. The South was losing the war.

On April 9, 1865, the **Confederate** General Robert E. Lee **surrendered** to General Grant at Appomattox Court House, Virginia. At last, the Civil War was over.

General Robert E. Lee

The United States during Lincoln's presidency

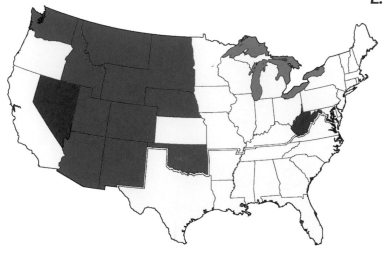

	Existing States		Existing Territories
	New States		

The Seven "Hats" of the U.S. President

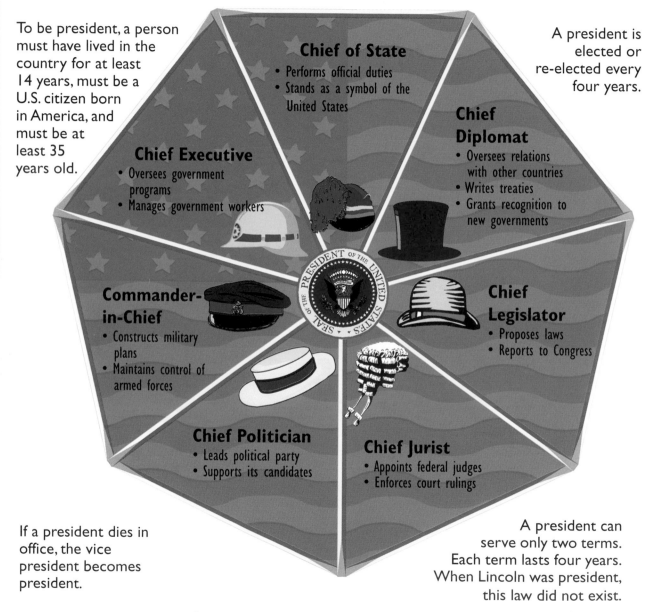

To be president, a person must have lived in the country for at least 14 years, must be a U.S. citizen born in America, and must be at least 35 years old.

A president is elected or re-elected every four years.

Chief of State
- Performs official duties
- Stands as a symbol of the United States

Chief Diplomat
- Oversees relations with other countries
- Writes treaties
- Grants recognition to new governments

Chief Executive
- Oversees government programs
- Manages government workers

Commander-in-Chief
- Constructs military plans
- Maintains control of armed forces

Chief Legislator
- Proposes laws
- Reports to Congress

Chief Politician
- Leads political party
- Supports its candidates

Chief Jurist
- Appoints federal judges
- Enforces court rulings

If a president dies in office, the vice president becomes president.

A president can serve only two terms. Each term lasts four years. When Lincoln was president, this law did not exist.

As president, Abraham Lincoln had seven jobs.

The Three Branches of the U.S. Government

Congress is in the Capitol Building in Washington, D.C. It can pass laws and stop the president's veto. Congress can also change the Constitution to stop the president's plans or Supreme Court rulings.

The president lives in the White House in Washington, D.C. He or she can stop (veto) laws passed by Congress, and propose new laws. The president can also choose Supreme Court judges.

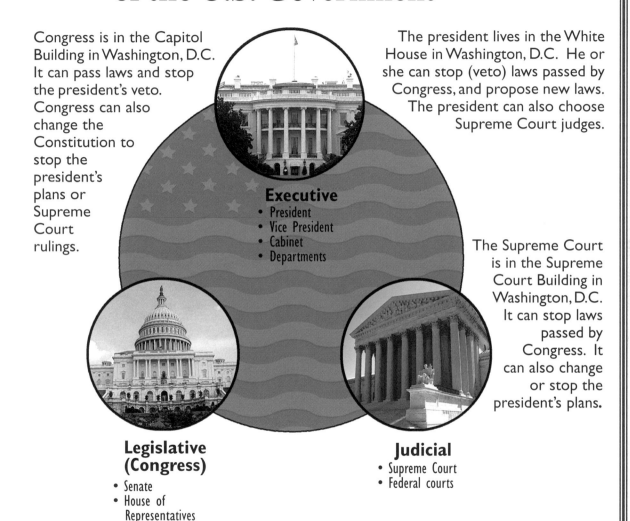

Executive
- President
- Vice President
- Cabinet
- Departments

The Supreme Court is in the Supreme Court Building in Washington, D.C. It can stop laws passed by Congress. It can also change or stop the president's plans.

Legislative (Congress)
- Senate
- House of Representatives

Judicial
- Supreme Court
- Federal courts

The U.S. Constitution formed three government branches. Each branch has power over the others. So, no single group or person can control the country. The Constitution calls this "separation of powers."

A Nation Mourns

*B*efore the end of the war, President Lincoln made plans to bring the southern states back into the **Union**. The period after the war when the country was reunited is called Reconstruction.

Lincoln favored a plan that would allow **seceded** states back into the Union. But some Republicans wanted to punish the South and make it pay for the war. And they wanted all Southern states to **ratify** the Thirteenth **Amendment**. The plan for Reconstruction remained unsettled.

On April 14, 1865, President Lincoln and his wife went to Ford's Theater with Major Henry R. Rathbone and his girlfriend Clara Harris. While Lincoln was watching the play *My American Cousin*, John Wilkes Booth shot him in the head.

Booth was a **Confederate** supporter. He was upset that the South had lost the war. He blamed Lincoln for the nation's problems. He and several other men had planned to kill President Lincoln, Vice President Andrew Johnson, General Grant, and Secretary of War Edwin Stanton.

John Wilkes Booth

Lincoln's box seat at Ford's Theater

Lincoln was rushed to a hotel room across the street. Six doctors worked to save his life. But the next day, at 7:22 P.M., he died. He was 56 years old.

Police caught Booth in a barn in Virginia. He was shot and killed. Others involved in the plan **surrendered** and were found guilty of murder. Some went to jail for life and others were **executed**.

The nation mourned the death of President Lincoln. He was a strong, **compassionate** leader who governed the country through the dark days of civil war. His work to end slavery and preserve the Union have made him one of the nation's most important presidents.

The Lincoln Memorial in Washington, D.C.

Glossary

Amendment - a law added to the U.S. Constitution.

ban - to forbid or prohibit.

border states - the states on the border between the North and the South. Delaware, Maryland, Kentucky, and Missouri were loyal to the North but still had slavery in the Civil War.

campaign - an organized series of events to get a candidate elected to office. A campaign is also a series of military operations with a specific goal.

candidate - a person who is seeking an office or position.

circuit - a district assigned to a judge for holding court.

commissioner - an official in charge of a government department.

company - a military unit made up of two or more platoons that forms part of a battalion.

compassionate - feeling sympathy for someone.

Confederate States of America - the country formed by the states of South Carolina, Georgia, Florida, Alabama, Louisiana, Mississippi, Texas, Virginia, Tennessee, Arkansas, and North Carolina that left the Union between 1860 and 1861. Also called the Confederacy.

Congress - the lawmaking body of the U.S. It is made up of the Senate and the House of Representatives.

conscription - forced enrollment by law in a country's armed forces.

Constitution - the laws that govern the United States.

debate - to discuss a question or topic, often publicly.

discharge - to be released from service.

elect - to choose by voting. A person chosen twice in a row for the same office is re-elected.

execute - to put to death in accordance with the law.

ferry - to carry across a narrow body of water in a boat or other craft.

House of Representatives - a group elected by Americans to help decide laws for the whole country; its members are called representatives.

legislature - the lawmaking group of a state or country. A legislator is someone who makes and passes laws.

militia - citizens trained for war or emergencies; the National Guard.

perish - to die.

platform - a public statement of principles of a politician or political party.

port - the place next to the land where ships come in from the ocean.

preliminary - coming before the main event.

proclamation - an official public announcement.

ratify - to officially approve.

rural - out in the country, not in the city.

secede - to break away; in 1860 and 1861, some southern states seceded from the United States.

Senate - one of the houses of Congress. Each state has two senators.

shackled - restrained by iron bands around the wrists and ankles that are often connected by a chain.

surrender - to give up.

surveyor - a person who determines the shape, area, and boundaries of a piece of land by taking measurements.

Union - the northern states in the country that stayed part of the United States when southern states were seceding.

Whig - a political party that was very strong in the early 1800s, but ended in the 1850s. They supported laws that helped business.

Internet Sites

The Presidents of the United States of America
http://www.whitehouse.gov/WH/glimpse/presidents/html/presidents.html
Part of the White House Web site.

Lincoln Home National Historic Site: http://www.nps.gov/liho/
Sponsored by the National Park Service.

Mr. Lincoln's Virtual Library: http://lcweb2.loc.gov/ammem/alhtml/
Sponsored by the Library of Congress.

These sites are subject to change. Go to your favorite search engine and type in United States Presidents for more sites.

Index